A Look At...

Wonders of the World

WORLD
BOOK

a Scott Fetzer company
Chicago
www.worldbookonline.com

CONTENTS

There is a glossary on page 62. Terms defined in the glossary are in type **that looks like this** on their first appearance on any spread (two facing pages).

Introducing the Wonders of the World

Imagine you are showing a visitor from another planet around our world. What to see? Where to go?

The Great Pyramid, built about 4,500 years ago, is one of the most famous structures on Earth.

Wonders of the Ancient World

More than 2,000 years ago, people in ancient Greece and Rome made listings of notable places for travelers to visit. Only objects made by human beings appeared on these lists, including **tombs** (burial places), **temples** (buildings for religious services), statues, and other structures that were very large, beautiful, costly, or unusual in some other way. Natural features of Earth, such as mountains, waterfalls, and caves, were not included.

Seven wonders

Seven of these ancient "wonders" were generally listed. They were built between 3000 B.C. and A.D. 476, and we now know them as the Seven Wonders of the Ancient World. To see them, tourists of old had to travel across Mediterranean Europe, North Africa, and western Asia. This was the **civilized** world known to the Greeks and **Romans** (people of Rome). The rest of the world was left out. Had they been aware of the Great Wall of China, they would have surely added an Eighth Wonder.

The Grand Canyon in the United States is one of the natural wonders of the world.

Seven Wonders of the Ancient World

- The pyramids of Egypt at Giza
- The Hanging Gardens of Babylon (modern Iraq)
- The Temple of Artemis at Ephesus (modern Turkey)
- The statue of Zeus at Olympia in Greece
- The Mausoleum at Halicarnassus (modern Turkey)
- The Colossus on the island of Rhodes in the Aegean Sea
- The Lighthouse of Alexandria in Egypt

The locations of the Seven Wonders of the Ancient World are shown by the red dots. The pyramids at Giza stand beside the Nile River in Egypt.

What makes a wonder?

Of the Seven Wonders of the Ancient World, only the pyramids of Egypt remain in anything like their original glory. People still come from all over the world to see them. But today, people also marvel at such natural wonders as the Grand Canyon in Arizona, as well as such old and beautiful buildings as the Taj Mahal in India. A wonder is any sight that makes people stop and stare in awe.

Natural wonders

In modern times, people have made lists of natural wonders to help us appreciate the beauty and variety of Earth's landscape. Microscopes and other human inventions allow us to see even the miniature wonders of nature, such as the pattern of a snowflake or the structure of a leaf. Human beings still add to the landscape with wonders of their own, such as skyscrapers, bridges, and **monuments** (structures built to honor a person or event).

Wonders all around

The more you look around you, the more wonders you'll see in the world. This book will introduce you to just a few of them. We'll begin in Egypt, more than 4,000 years ago, when the pyramids were new.

The Pyramids of Egypt

The pyramids of Egypt are the oldest of the Seven Wonders of the Ancient World. They have survived the passing centuries.

Top of the list

The pyramids were the biggest of all the Seven Wonders. The largest pyramid stands about 450 feet (137 meters) high, though some of its upper stones are gone now. Its base covers about 13 acres (5 hectares). Even people who had seen the marvels of ancient Greece, Rome, and Babylon came away impressed from a visit to the pyramids.

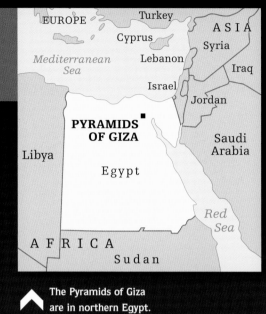

The Pyramids of Giza are in northern Egypt.

The first pyramid in ancient Egypt was built for King Zoser about 2650 B.C. It was called the Step Pyramid because it rises in a series of giant steps. It stands at the site of the ancient city of Memphis, at Saqqarah, near Cairo.

The pyramids of Giza

The pyramids were built as **tombs** for kings of Egypt. (A tomb is any structure built primarily to hold human remains.) Each pyramid had a square base and four smooth, triangular-shaped sides. The **ruins** (remains) of 35 large pyramids can be seen today near the Nile River in Egypt. But the most famous are three large pyramids at Giza *(GEE zuh)* near Cairo. These pyramids were built about 2600 to 2500 B.C. for three powerful kings.

Did You Know?

The ancient **Romans** were impressed by the size of the pyramids in Egypt. However, they also thought that the pyramids were a waste of money dreamed up by Egyptian kings with nothing better to do.

The pyramids of Giza are the best preserved of the Seven Wonders of the Ancient World. The three largest were built for King Khufu, King Khafre, and King Menkaure.

Building the Pyramids

Building a pyramid was a big project. The builders did not consider the cost or how much time it took. They believed they were building for eternity.

The Great Pyramid

The largest pyramid in ancient Egypt was built for King Khufu, who lived about 2600 B.C. More than 2 million stone blocks were piled up to make the **tomb.** Each block weighed about 2½ tons (2.3 metric tons)!

The builders

No one knows how long it took to build a pyramid. As many as 100,000 workers were brought in from the farms along the Nile River. They worked on the project for three or four months each year during periods when the floodwaters of the Nile covered their fields and made farming impossible.

The huge stones were cut and shaped with chisels and saws. Workers pulled the blocks of stone onto wooden sledges (sleds).

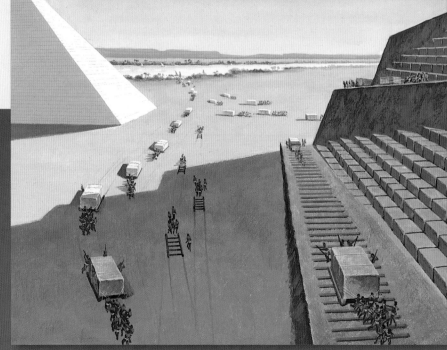

Groups of workers dragged the sledges up ramps on the pyramid. They put logs beneath the stones to reduce friction (rubbing together) and make the sledges easier to move. The ramps were built higher and higher as the pyramid grew. A finished pyramid, shining white in the sun, can be seen on the left. ➤

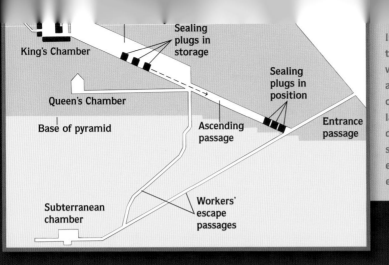

King's Chamber

Sealing plugs in storage

Sealing plugs in position

Queen's Chamber

Entrance passage

Base of pyramid

Ascending passage

Subterranean chamber

Workers' escape passages

Inside the Great Pyramid, a passage called the Grand Gallery led to the King's Chamber, where the king was buried. Below this was a room called the Queen's Chamber, but no one was buried here. After the king's burial, large blocks called sealing plugs were slid down the passage from the Grand Gallery, sealing the tomb so that no robbers could enter. Workers left the tomb through an escape passageway.

How the pyramids were built

The pyramid builders had no machinery or iron tools. They cut the huge blocks of stone with copper chisels and saws. Most of the stones came from nearby quarries—places where stone is dug or cut out for building. Others were brought by boat along the Nile River.

Gangs of workers dragged the stones up long ramps of earth and brick to form the layers of the pyramid that slowly rose higher and higher. Finally, they covered the pyramid with smooth white stones. These stones were placed so carefully that, from a distance, the pyramid appeared to have been cut from a single white stone.

Most of the outer stones are now gone, except for a few at the base of the Great Pyramid. But when they were new, the brilliant white pyramids must have been an amazing sight.

American Pyramids

Almost 2,000 years ago, people of Mexico and Central America built massive stepped pyramids with **temples** on top. The Pyramid of the Sun at Teotihuacán (*tay oh tee wah KAHN*), near what is now Mexico City, has a larger base than the largest pyramid in Egypt. Ancient people in Peru also built pyramids.

The Pyramid of the Sun at Teotihuacán in Mexico once had a temple on its top. This pyramid is more than 1,500 years old.

More Wonders of Egypt

Egypt has other ancient wonders. Four thousand years ago, people came to stare at the Great Sphinx, a mysterious statue in the desert near Giza. Today, people still puzzle over this strange monument.

The Great Sphinx has been worn away by sand, wind, rain, and sun. Part of the head is broken. Some historians believe that gunners of the French general Napoleon blasted it with cannons (large guns) for "fun" when the French invaded Egypt in 1798.

Land of the Nile

Egypt was the birthplace of one of the world's first **civilizations** (organized societies). People from other lands were impressed by the **fertile** land beside the Nile River, which was well suited for growing crops. They were also impressed by the large reed boats sailing on the river, and especially by the huge **temples** and statues.

The Black Land

The mighty Nile River was the lifeblood of ancient Egypt. Every year, the river overflowed and left a layer of rich, black soil along its banks. Farmers planted crops in this fertile soil and enjoyed large harvests. Because of its life-giving black soil, the ancient Egyptians called their country Kemet, meaning "Black Land."

The Nile River enabled farmers to grow huge supplies of food. The Nile also provided water for irrigation and served as ancient Egypt's main transportation route.

Huge stone statues of King Ramses II guarded the Great Temple at Abu Simbel near the Nile River for more than 3,000 years. When the Aswan High Dam was built in the 1960's, builders moved the temple to higher ground to escape the dam's rising waters.

The mysterious Sphinx

Artists in ancient Egypt carved large stone statues to represent kings or gods. There were many stone sphinxes *(sfihngkses)*—imaginary creatures of ancient myths (stories). The most remarkable was the Great Sphinx.

The Great Sphinx may represent a king or a god. It has a human head and the body of a lion. The Sphinx wears a royal headdress—a decoration for the head—and lies near the pyramid of King Khafre, the second of the three largest pyramids at Giza. Some historians claim the face of the Sphinx may be the king's likeness, but others believe the Great Sphinx is even older than the pyramids.

Sphinx Facts

- The Great Sphinx is 240 feet (73 meters) long and about 66 feet (20 meters) high.

- The head and body were carved out of a giant **limestone** rock. Smaller blocks of the same rock were used to build several pyramids.

- The paws and legs were made from stone blocks.

- Sand has often buried the Great Sphinx up to its neck! Workers last cleared away the sand in 1938.

The tombs of Egyptian kings were packed with treasures. Most of the riches were soon carried off by robbers. But one tomb was overlooked and later became a new wonder of the world.

Mummies and treasure

The Egyptians believed in life after death and made careful preparations for death and burial. They believed it was important to preserve the body of a dead person, which they did through mummification. In this process, a body is treated with chemicals and oils and then dried to prevent it from decaying. Then it is wrapped in cloth bandages and put inside a coffin.

Ancient Egyptians placed mummies inside a **tomb.** A tomb also held many items the dead person would need in the afterlife, including wigs and food. The tomb of a king was filled with treasures of gold, jewels, furniture, and other precious objects.

A magnificent gold death mask covered the head and shoulders of Tutankhamun's mummy.

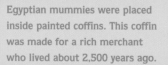

Egyptian mummies were placed inside painted coffins. This coffin was made for a rich merchant who lived about 2,500 years ago.

This throne was found in Tutankhamun's tomb—the only tomb of an ancient Egyptian king to be discovered almost completely undamaged.

Valley of the Kings

Tutankhamun's tomb is 1 of more than 60 royal tombs in or near the Valley of the Kings, a narrow rocky valley on the west bank of the Nile River. The tombs are in the form of corridors (long hallways) and rooms cut into rock. The largest tomb was discovered in 1995.

Tomb robbers

After the burial, the tomb was sealed. But this failed to keep out determined robbers. Thieves broke into most of the pyramids and stole their treasures. After about 1700 B.C., Egyptian kings stopped building pyramids and dug out secret tombs in cliffs instead.

Tomb of the boy king

Tutankhamun *(TOOT ahngk AH muhn)* became king of Egypt about 1332 B.C., when he was only about 9 years old. He died when he was about 18 and was buried in the Valley of the Kings, near the city of Thebes *(theebz)*.

His tomb remained undiscovered until 1922, when the British **archaeologist** Howard Carter discovered it. (An archaeologist studies the people, customs, and life of ancient times.) It had not been opened since ancient times and still contained most of its treasures. Its four rooms contained more than 5,000 objects, including chests, beds, necklaces, **chariots** (two-wheeled carriages pulled by horses), swords, ostrich feathers, models of ships, toys, and jars of precious oils.

Queen Nefertiti *(NEHF uhr TEE tee)* was the wife of Akhenaten *(AH kuh NAH tehn)*, who was king of Egypt before Tutankhamun. This painted sculpture of Nefertiti was made about 1355 B.C. by an unknown Egyptian artist. Akhenaten and Tutankhamun were probably relatives.

and Ephesus

Babylon and Ephesus were great cities of the ancient world. Today, we can only imagine what the wonders of these cities may have looked like.

The Hanging Gardens

No one is sure what the Hanging Gardens looked like. They were probably built by King Nebuchadnezzar *(nehb uh kuhd NEHZ uhr)* II for one of his wives. Babylon was a rich kingdom in what is now Iraq, near the modern city of Baghdad.

All that we know about the Hanging Gardens comes from the writings of a priest named Berossus who lived in Babylon in the 200's B.C. He described gardens laid out on a brick terrace (outdoor space) about 400 feet (120 meters) square and 75 feet (23 meters) above the ground. To water the flowers and trees in the gardens, slaves worked in shifts, turning screws to lift water from the Euphrates River.

According to one story, Nebuchadnezzar II married a mountain princess and built the Hanging Gardens so that she would feel at home.

 The Hanging Gardens grew on the roof of a high building near Nebuchadnezzar's palace

Babylon was an ancient city on the banks of the Euphrates River in present-day Iraq. Today, **ruins** can be seen among modern buildings.

The Temple of Artemis

One of the largest **temples** built in ancient times stood in the Greek city of Ephesus *(EHF ih suhs)* on the west coast of what is now Turkey. It was made entirely of marble—a costly stone—except for the roof, which was made of wood and covered with tiles.

The temple was built about 550 B.C. and dedicated to the Greek goddess Artemis *(AHR tuh mihs)*. In Greek mythology (collected stories), Artemis was the daughter of Zeus, king of the gods. She was the goddess of childbirth and of wild animals and hunting.

An impressive feature of the temple was the 106 columns, each about 67 feet (20 meters) high. These columns were a gift from King Croesus of Lydia (a country in ancient Asia Minor). Croesus was famous for his wealth.

Remains?

Nothing remains of the Hanging Gardens. The Temple of Artemis burned in 356 B.C. A second temple on the same foundation also burned in A.D. 262. Only the foundation and parts of this second temple remain. Sculptures from the second temple can be seen in the British Museum in London.

The Temple of Artemis was famous for its decoration and plentiful use of marble.

Did You Know?

- The walls of Nebuchadnezzar's Babylon were almost 85 feet (26 meters) thick.

- A wide moat (ditch filled with water) surrounded the walls.

- The Tower of Babel, described in the Bible, was in Babylon. It was a terraced pyramid, or ziggurat, in the city's temple area. The Tower is shown beside the Euphrates River in the illustration on page 14.

Greek Wonders

The ancient Greeks, known for their beautiful buildings and sculptures, built five of the Wonders of the Ancient World.

The Statue of Zeus

People came to Olympia for the Olympic Games, first held in 776 B.C. In a great **temple**, visitors were amazed by a 43-foot- (13-meter-) high statue of Zeus, king of the gods. The figure was made about 430 B.C. by Phidias *(FIHD ee uhs)*, the greatest sculptor of ancient Greece. (A sculptor is an artist who makes figures.)

The Statue of Zeus at Olympia had a wooden core, partially covered in gold. The artist made the god's flesh from ivory.

The Temple of Hephaestus in Athens, Greece, was probably built about 450 B.C.

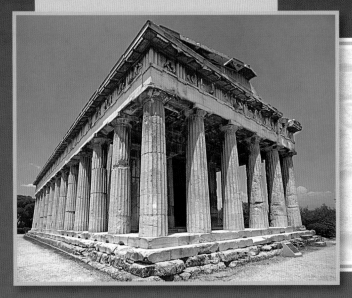

Graceful Greeks

Classical Greek buildings made much use of colonnades—rows of elegant columns that supported the roof. A Greek temple usually had rows of columns around a long, inner room. Such Greek sculptors as Phidias were masters at making lifelike figures of gods and goddesses, usually covered in marble.

The Mausoleum at Halicarnassus

A huge, white marble **tomb** was built about 353 B.C. in what is now southwestern Turkey. It was made for Mausolus, ruler of a province (territory) in the **Persian Empire.** Ancient Persia included parts of what are now Iran and Afghanistan. Two Greek architects, Satyros and Pythios, designed the tomb. Four Greek sculptors—Bryaxis, Leochares, Scopas, and Timotheus—carved the decorated band, or frieze *(freez)*, on the building.

The Mausoleum *(MAW suh LEE uhm)* was about 150 feet (46 meters) high. A series of 36 columns supported a pyramid, on top of which was probably a statue of Mausolus in a **chariot.** The tomb was so impressive that all large tombs came to be called mausoleums.

Remains?

The Statue of Zeus no longer exists. In fact, none of Phidias's statues survive. The top part of the Mausoleum was destroyed by an earthquake, and only pieces of the building and its decorations remain. Some sculptures from the Mausoleum can be seen in the British Museum in London.

The Mausoleum at Halicarnassus was a great marble tomb. Some of the most famous Greek sculptors and artists worked on this building.

Colossus and Lighthouse

In ancient times, passengers aboard ships sailing the Aegean and Mediterranean seas saw two wondrous landmarks— a giant statue and a towering lighthouse. These, too, were among the Seven Wonders of the Ancient World.

The Colossus of Rhodes

Near the harbor of Rhodes, an island in the Aegean *(ee JEE uhn)* Sea, stood a huge statue. It showed the sun god Helios and stood about 110 feet (34 meters) tall. The Greek sculptor Chares worked on the figure from about 294 to 282 B.C. He used stone blocks and several tons of iron bars to hold up the hollow figure cast in bronze sections.

Did You Know?

A colossus is any gigantic statue. We call something that is really enormous "colossal." The ancient **Romans** called their huge arena in Rome the Colosseum. The people of Rhodes built their Colossus statue in thanksgiving after they survived a yearlong attack by an army of Macedonians (people of Macedonia, a country in southeastern Europe).

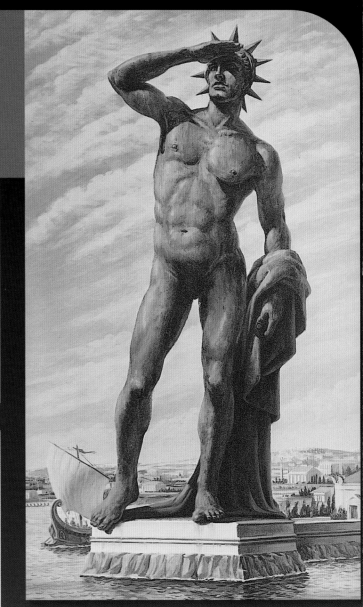

The Colossus of Rhodes was a statue of the sun god. No one is sure exactly what the figure looked like, but it was almost as tall as the Statue of Liberty. The giant structure probably stood beside the harbor.

The Lighthouse of Alexandria

On the island of Pharos in the harbor of Alexandria, Egypt, stood a magnificent lighthouse. It was so famous in the ancient world that the word *pharos* came to mean "lighthouse." The Alexandrian lighthouse was built between 283 and 246 B.C., from a design by the Greek architect Sostratos.

The lighthouse had three sections. The base was square, the middle section was eight-sided, and the top section was round. A fire burning at the top of the lighthouse gave light that could be seen for miles.

Remains?

In 226 B.C., the Colossus was toppled by an earthquake. The metal supports remained for more than 800 years until they were sold for scrap in A.D. 653. An earthquake also brought down the Lighthouse of Alexandria after it had stood for about 1,500 years.

Vanished wonders

Six of the ancient world's Seven Wonders were lost. Only the pyramids remain for us to see. However, today we have the means to uncover remains of lost cities and to recapture some of the glories of past **civilizations.**

The Lighthouse of Alexandria, the first important lighthouse in the world, stood over 440 feet (134 meters) high. Its fiery light guided ships into the city's harbor.

Lost Cities

Over the centuries, civilizations and cities have flourished and fallen. Today, only ruins are left to hint at their vanished wonders.

Petra was an ancient city in what is now Jordan. Trade flourished in Petra for about 600 years between the late 400's B.C. and the early A.D. 200's. The people cut deeply into cliffs to make their **temples** and houses. Petra has been called the "rose-red city" because of its red stone buildings and the red cliffs that surround it.

Pompeii, the buried city

Of all the world's lost cities, Pompeii *(pom PAY)* in Italy is perhaps the most famous. It was a resort city as well as a port—a place where ships and boats could load and unload goods. It was also close to the foot of Mount Vesuvius *(vuh SOO vee uhs)*, a volcano. Rich **Romans** built comfortable homes near the seashore. There were farms, orchards, a market, and factories that made fish sauce, cloth, and perfumes.

All this vanished in the summer of A.D. 79, when Vesuvius suddenly erupted. Lava and mud covered the nearby city of Herculaneum *(HUR kyuh LAY nee uhm)*. Hot ashes, stones, and cinders rained down on Pompeii. Many people were buried in their houses. Others were killed by poisonous gases and fumes.

Pompeii was buried by a volcano in A.D. 79 and was not rediscovered until the 1700's. Today, much of the city has been uncovered.

A city no more

Pompeii was completely buried. Only the tops of walls and columns showed above the waste. The survivors dug out as many valuables as they could, but the city was gone.

Pompeii remained buried for nearly 1,700 years. From time to time, local people dug into the **ruins** searching for buried treasure, but serious investigation did not begin until 1748, when a peasant dug into a buried wall. By the 1900's, **archaeologists** had uncovered much of the city and restored many streets and buildings.

Pompeii today

Today, visitors to Pompeii walk in and out of houses and up and down narrow lanes, just as the Pompeiians did. They can see election slogans written on the walls of houses. (The disaster happened during a local election campaign.)

Pompeii has yielded many domestic items that show us how people lived in a Roman city. There are human remains, too. As the ash hardened around buried bodies, a mold was formed. Then the bodies decayed, leaving a hollow shell. By carefully filling the shells with plaster, archaeologists have made detailed copies of the bodies.

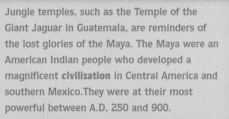

Jungle temples, such as the Temple of the Giant Jaguar in Guatemala, are reminders of the lost glories of the Maya. The Maya were an American Indian people who developed a magnificent **civilization** in Central America and southern Mexico. They were at their most powerful between A.D. 250 and 900.

Ancient Walls

In ancient times, walls were built around cities to protect the citizens from enemies. Walls were even built across mountains!

The Great Wall of China

The Great Wall is the longest structure ever built. It was originally constructed to protect ancient China against invaders from the north. In the 200's B.C., the Chinese emperor Shi Huangdi ordered earlier walls to be linked by new walls and forts. The Great Wall follows a winding course for about 5,500 miles (8,850 kilometers) over mountains and hills and along the edges of deserts.

Hadrian's Wall

The **Romans** built Hadrian's Wall, across 73 miles (118 kilometers) of northern England. In the A.D. 120's, the Roman Emperor Hadrian ordered the construction of the wall to defend the frontier of Britain from the Picts—the people of Scotland in the north. The remains of forts and stretches of the wall still stand.

The Western Wall in Jerusalem—also known as the Wailing Wall—is a Jewish holy place. About 2,000 years ago, it served as a retaining wall around the mount, or hill, upon which the Jew's holy **temple** stood. The wall is about 160 feet (49 meters) long and 40 feet (12 meters) high. Today, Jews come to the wall to pray, and it has become a symbol of Jewish unity and survival.

The Great Wall was built to defend China against invaders.

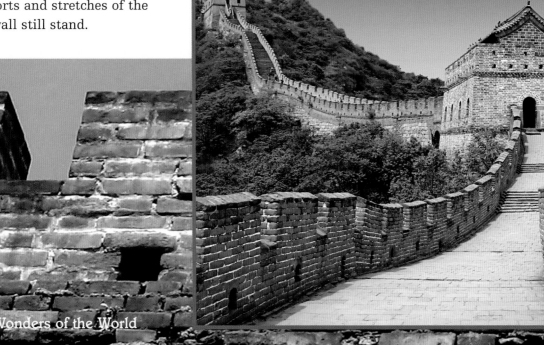

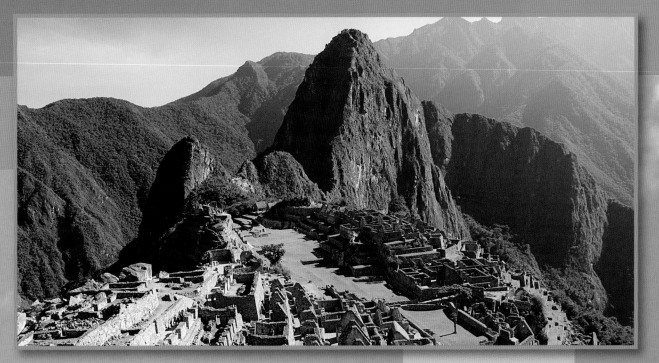

Machu Picchu was a city built by the Inca of Peru.

Great Zimbabwe

The walls of Great Zimbabwe *(zihm BAH bway)* in Africa are made of granite, a hard stone. The walls were built after A.D. 1000 by the Shona people. The word *zimbabwe* means "house of stone" in the Shona language. The **ruins** include part of a wall up to 36 feet (11 meters) high and 800 feet (240 meters) long.

Great Zimbabwe was an ancient African city.

Machu Picchu

The ruins of the walled Inca city of Machu Picchu *(MAH choo PEEK choo)* lie in the mountains near Cusco in Peru. The Inca were a native South American people who ruled one of the largest and richest empires in the Americas. The Inca were conquered by the Spaniards in the 1530's. Machu Picchu was one of the last Inca strongholds.

Majestic Canyon

The Grand Canyon in Arizona is a natural wonder of the world—a mile-deep gash in the earth where the rocks seem to change color throughout the day. The Grand Canyon is included on most lists of the seven natural wonders of the world.

River power

The Grand Canyon is a valley about 277 miles (446 kilometers) long and from 1 to 18 miles (1.6 to 29 kilometers) wide. The Colorado River flows through the canyon, providing an impressive example of the power of water to shape the land. The mighty Colorado carved out the canyon over millions of years by cutting through layers of rocks.

The Colorado River wore away rock layers bit by bit to form the Grand Canyon. In places, the river has cut its way more than 7,000 feet (2,100 meters) down.

Cactuses grow throughout the Grand Canyon, especially in low areas. >

Changing colors

The rocks of the Grand Canyon have different shades and seem to change color throughout the day. A good time to see the canyon is at sunset, when the red and brown layers are especially brilliant.

History

Fossils found in the canyon tell us what animals and plants lived there millions of years ago. During the last 4,000 years, various Native American groups made their home there. In 1540, Spanish explorers were the first Europeans to see its wonders. In 1869, John Wesley Powell led a river journey through the large canyon to study its geology (rocks and soil). He gave the Grand Canyon its name.

Seven Natural Wonders

These places are sometimes included on lists of the seven natural wonders of the world:

- The Grand Canyon in the United States
- Victoria Falls, a waterfall in Africa
- The Great Barrier Reef near Australia
- The Harbor of Rio de Janeiro in Brazil
- Mount Everest in Asia
- Paricutín, a volcano in Mexico
- The aurora borealis, also known as the Northern Lights

Grand Canyon Facts

- Some rocks in the Grand Canyon are 2 billion years old.
- The bottom of the canyon is warmer and drier than the top.
- Cactuses grow throughout the canyon, especially in low areas.
- About 300 different kinds of birds live in the Grand Canyon area, along with about 120 other kinds of animals, including beaver, bighorn sheep, deer, and mountain lion. The pink Grand Canyon rattlesnake is found only in the canyon area.

The Grand Canyon is home to many kinds of animals, including herds of desert bighorn sheep.

Mighty Falls

What makes a thunderous waterfall plunge over cliffs? In wearing away its channel, a river uncovers some rock layers that are softer than others. River water wears away soft rock more quickly than hard rock. If the water moves from hard rock upstream to softer rock downstream, the soft rock is worn away faster—and the water falls.

The thundering Victoria Falls is on the Zambia-Zimbabwe border in Africa.

Victoria Falls

Many waterfalls are dramatic, but Victoria Falls in southern Africa is one of the most thrilling sights in the world. There, the Zambezi River, about 5,604 feet (1,708 meters) wide at the falls, drops suddenly into a deep, narrow opening in the earth. In the center of the falls, the river drops 355 feet (108 meters) into the gorge—a deep, narrow valley.

The local name of the falls—Mosi-oa-Tunya ("smoke that thunders")—describes the tremendous sound and the clouds of water vapor. The mist and spray can be seen from a great distance. British explorer David Livingstone sighted Victoria Falls in 1885 and named it in honor of Queen Victoria of the United Kingdom.

The spectacular Iguaçu Falls lies on the border between Brazil and Argentina. It is about 2 miles (3 kilometers) wide and made up of 275 separate waterfalls.

Niagara Falls is on the Niagara River, about halfway between Lake Erie and Lake Ontario. The Horseshoe Falls (left) is on the Canadian side of the border in the province of Ontario.

Niagara Falls

Niagara Falls is one of the most spectacular natural wonders of North America. At the falls, the Niagara River, which forms part of the United States-Canadian border, plunges into a deep gorge. Niagara Falls is actually two waterfalls—the Horseshoe Falls, which is in Canada, and the American Falls, which is in the United States.

The Horseshoe Falls is about 167 feet (51 meters) high and 2,600 feet (792 meters) wide at its widest point. The American Falls is about 176 feet (54 meters) high and 1,000 feet (305 meters) wide. Below the falls, sightseers can travel in boats to get close to the churning waters.

Angel Falls, in Venezuela, is the highest waterfall in the world. It has a total height of 3,212 feet (979 meters). Its longest unbroken drop is 2,648 feet (807 meters). Jimmy Angel, an American pilot, was the first known non-native person to sight the falls, when he flew over it in 1935 while searching for gold.

and Its Shores

The ocean contains fascinating underwater worlds that are home to thousands of different sea creatures. Along its shorelines, the majesty of the sea and land create landscapes of spectacular natural beauty.

The Great Barrier Reef stretches along the northeast coast of Australia.

The Great Barrier Reef

The Great Barrier Reef is the world's largest group of coral reefs. A coral reef is a **limestone** formation that lies under or just above the surface of the ocean. The coral is made of the hardened skeletons of dead water animals called polyps *(POL ihps)*. Billions of living polyps are attached to the reef.

An undersea garden

The colorful corals of the Great Barrier Reef make a lovely sea garden for a great variety of sea creatures. The reef is home to about 1,500 different kinds of fish. Crabs, giant clams, sea turtles, and many kinds of birds also live on the reef and its islands.

The beauty of its corals makes the Great Barrier Reef a unique wonder of the world. The reef is home to hundreds of different kinds of fish and other sea animals.

A prehistoric wonder

The Great Barrier Reef has been growing for millions of years. The reef now extends in a broken chain for about 1,400 miles (2,300 kilometers) along the northeast coast of Australia. Most of the reef is a national park visited by tourists from all over the world.

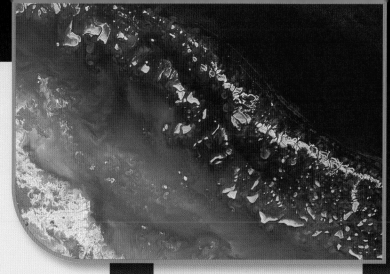

The Great Barrier Reef is made up of more than 3,000 individual reefs and about 1,000 islands. About 400 kinds of corals occur on the reef.

The Harbor of Rio de Janeiro

The Harbor of Rio de Janeiro in Brazil is a bay—a part of a sea or lake extending into the land. It is called "arm of the sea" by local people.

The Harbor of Rio de Janeiro is the largest bay in the world based on volume of water. Portuguese sailors discovered the bay in the early 1500's. Slipping through a narrow opening in the coastline, they arrived at a calm body of water they mistook for the mouth of a great river. They named the area Rio de Janeiro, Portuguese for "River of January," in honor of the month they arrived. The city of Rio de Janeiro grew along the harbor.

Today, Rio de Janeiro is the second largest city of Brazil and one of the chief seaports in South America. It ranks as an important center of finance, trade, and transportation.

The Harbor of Rio de Janeiro in Brazil is a natural bay surrounded by spectacular mountains and rock formations. ▼

From the wonders of the deep ocean to the highest mountain peak, people have explored the marvels of Earth. Since ancient times, they have woven stories around mountains— distant, beautiful, and often dangerous.

A mountain may stand as an isolated peak, or it may form part of a mountain range, such as the Rocky Mountains in North America. The Rockies stretch for more than 3,000 miles (4,800 kilometers) through the United States and Canada.

Mount Everest

The height of a mountain is usually given as the distance its peak rises above sea level. The world's highest mountain is Mount Everest, located in the Himalaya mountain system. It rises 29,035 feet (8,850 meters) above sea level on the border of Nepal and Tibet.

Mount Everest was named for Sir George Everest, a British surveyor-general of India in the 1800's. Many climbers have tried to scale Mount Everest since the British first saw it in the 1850's. Avalanches, crevasses, and strong winds combine with extreme steepness and thin air to make the climb difficult.

Another Himalayan peak, K2 (also called Mount Godwin Austen or Dapsang), is only slightly lower than Everest. It is the second highest mountain in the world.

Highest of all Earth's mountains is Mount Everest in the Himalaya, the greatest range of mountains on Earth. Everest was first climbed in 1953. Since then, many adventurous people have stood on its snow-covered peak.

Mount Fuji stands 12,388 feet (3,776 meters) tall. It lies on the island of Honshu, about 60 miles (97 kilometers) southwest of Tokyo.

Sacred mountains

Some mountains are held **sacred** (holy) by local people. Many Japanese believe that Mount Fuji, the highest mountain in Japan, is a holy mountain. More than 50,000 pilgrims (religious travelers) climb to the top every year.

Home of the gods

The top of Mount Olympus, the highest mountain in Greece, is usually covered with snow and hidden in clouds. The ancient Greeks believed Olympus was the home of the gods. People thought that Zeus, king of the gods, lived there with his family in a palace.

Ancient Greeks believed Zeus and 11 other gods and goddesses lived atop Mount Olympus. His 9 daughters were thought to live on the slopes of the mountain.

Volcanoes and Geysers

With its clouds of fire, rivers of lava, and missiles of molten rock, an erupting volcano is spectacular and terrifying!

Paricutín is the most recently formed volcanic mountain in the Western Hemisphere. It appeared in 1943 when lava began to erupt from a crack in a Mexican cornfield.

What is a volcano?

A volcano is an opening in Earth's surface. In an eruption, lava (hot, melted rock), hot gases, and chunks of rock burst out through the opening from deep inside Earth. The melted rock cools and hardens. In time, it may build up to form a cone-shaped mountain.

It's hard to imagine the power of a volcano. In 1815, Mount Tambora in Indonesia erupted, killing about 92,000 people. Scientists estimate that this volcano released 6 million times more energy than an atomic bomb.

Paricutín

Paricutín (*puh REE kuh TEEN*) is a volcano in the Mexican state of Michoacán. It is remarkable for the speed of its formation. Paricutín appeared as a long, narrow opening in a farmer's field on February 20, 1943. Within a year, it reached a height of 1,102 feet (336 meters). Paricutín's lava flows destroyed the towns of Paricutín and San Juan Parangaricutiro and damaged other villages. When Paricutín stopped erupting in 1952, it stood 1,391 feet (424 meters) high.

Did You Know?

Volcanic islands are actually the tops of undersea volcanoes. After repeated eruptions, these volcanoes grow big enough to reach the ocean's surface. Mauna Loa in Hawaii—the world's largest volcano—is higher than Mount Everest! It rises almost 30,000 feet (9,100 meters) from the floor of the Pacific Ocean. Only 13,677 feet (4,169 meters) of the volcano is above sea level.

Glowing red-hot lava flows from the Anak Krakatau volcano in Indonesia. Such events are the most spectacular fireworks displays on Earth.

A very big bang

One of the biggest volcanic eruptions in history was made in 1883 by the Krakatau *(krah kuh TOW)* volcano in Indonesia. When it erupted, the explosion was heard about 3,000 miles (4,800 kilometers) away. A cloud of dust was shot 17 miles (27 kilometers) into the air. This volcanic dust was blown around Earth several times, producing brilliant red sunsets in many parts of the world. Krakatau's eruption caused sea waves almost 130 feet (40 meters) high to sweep across nearby islands. About 36,000 people drowned.

Geysers

A geyser is a spring that blasts a jet of steaming hot water high into the air. Geysers are spectacular to watch—from a distance— and not as dangerous as volcanoes.

Old Faithful in Yellowstone National Park is probably the world's most famous geyser. Once about every 90 minutes, the geyser sends a stream of boiling water more than 100 feet (30 meters) into the air.

Volcanoes and Geysers **33**

Wonders in the Sky

For thousands of years, human beings have been awed by light displays in the night sky. Some of these wonders can only be seen from certain regions of the world. Others can be seen from anywhere on Earth.

Auroras

In Earth's polar regions, natural displays of colorful light called auroras extend across the sky. Auroras form when a flow of particles (tiny bits of matter) from the sun reaches Earth. The particles contain electrical energy. When these particles strike other particles that surround Earth, energy is released. Some of this energy appears in the form of auroras.

Auroras can be seen with the unaided eye only at night. The most common color in an aurora is green, but displays that occur extremely high in the sky may be red or purple.

Northern lights

Auroras in the northern part of the world are called the Northern Lights. The colored lights appear as curved lines, clouds, and streaks. Some auroras move or get brighter or flicker suddenly. The best time to see the Northern Lights is from December to March, when nights are longest and the sky is darkest.

Meteor showers, like this one over Beijing, China, occur when Earth travels through a stream of meteoroids.

The aurora borealis, also known as the Northern Lights, is a natural display of light. It is one of the natural wonders of the world.

Meteor Crater in Arizona is a huge hole left after a meteorite smashed into Earth.

Rocks from space

From any point on Earth, one can sometimes see sudden flashes of bright light in the sky when space rocks fall into the atmosphere. Meteors are bright streaks of light that appear for a very short time in the sky. They are often called shooting stars or falling stars, because they look like stars falling from the sky. The brightest meteors are sometimes called fireballs.

A meteor appears when a meteoroid—a piece of hard material—enters Earth's atmosphere (the air that surrounds Earth) from outer space. Air rubs against the meteoroid and heats it. This makes it glow. Most meteors glow for only about a second, but they leave a shining trail.

Meteoroids usually break up into tiny pieces before reaching Earth. Those that reach Earth are called meteorites. Meteorites reach Earth because they are the right size to travel through the atmosphere. If they are too small, they break up. If they are too big, they may explode. Most meteorites are quite small, about the size of a pebble.

Smash hit

Once in a while, a large meteorite hurtles right through Earth's atmosphere and hits the ground. The crash produces an impact crater—a bowl-shaped hole in the ground as big as 10 miles (25 kilometers) across. Scientists have found more than 120 such craters. Among the most famous is Meteor Crater in Arizona. This huge hole is about 4,180 feet (1,275 meters) wide and 570 feet (175 meters) deep! It was blasted out of the ground about 50,000 years ago when an iron meteorite of 300,000 tons (270,000 metric tons) or more struck Earth.

Ancient rocks help shape the landscape. Over many millions of years, rocks are often worn into strange shapes by wind, rain, and sun. The wearing away of rock also forms caves—hollow areas in the earth that contain underground passages and chambers.

Rounded limestone hills are found in China. These hills lie near the town of Yangshuo in the southern part of the country.

Uluru

Uluru, once known as Ayers Rock, is the world's largest monolith, or single large stone. It is often listed as one of the seven natural wonders of the world. This mass of reddish stone rises 1,100 feet (335 meters) above the desert in central Australia.

The Australian Aborigines, the first people of Australia, named the rock Uluru, meaning "great pebble." To them, the rock was a **sacred** place, and they decorated caves in the rock with paintings. In 1873, an explorer of European descent named the rock after Sir Henry Ayers, the chief government minister of South Australia.

Uluru is made of **sandstone**—a kind of rock made mostly of sand—that was formed more than 480 million years ago, when central Australia was covered by a shallow sea. From sunrise to sunset, the rock changes color with the changing light of the day.

The large mass of Uluru rises abruptly from the flat plains. The rock glows red during sunrise and sunset.

Caves

A cave is a naturally hollow area in the earth that is large enough for a person to enter. Most caves are formed in **limestone** or in a related rock, such as marble or dolomite. Over thousands of years, underground water slowly dissolves the rock, forming underground chambers and passageways.

Some caves have only one chamber, but others form a large network of passages and chambers. The Mammoth-Flint Ridge cave system in Kentucky is the longest cave ever explored. More than 300 miles (480 kilometers) of its passageways have been mapped, but geologists think that the cave system extends even farther.

Cave exploring

Long ago, people made their homes in caves. Today, people are more likely to go cave exploring. Cave exploring is exciting but risky. Cave explorers should always go in groups, headed by experienced leaders.

Caves are cold, damp, and dark. Explorers use a flashlight to see the strange landscapes of stalactites and stalagmites. These iciclelike formations are made by slow drips of water that contain **minerals,** which wear away the rock. Stalactites hang from the roof of a cave. Stalagmites are pillars that rise from the cave floor. Underground lakes, rivers, and waterfalls also flow through many caves.

Stalactites and stalagmites abound in Mammoth Cave in Kentucky.

Plant Wonders

Growing on Earth's surface are hundreds of thousands of different kinds of plants— each of them a wonder. No animal can match the biggest plant for size, and nothing on Earth lives as long as some plants.

Ancient giants

Millions of years ago, sequoia *(sih KWOY uh)* trees flourished in forests throughout much of the world. Today, only two kinds of true sequoias remain—the redwood and the giant sequoia. They grow chiefly in California. Their only close relative is a Chinese tree called the dawn redwood.

Redwoods grow up to 300 feet (91 meters) high, about as tall as a 30-story building. Giant sequoias are not that high, but their trunks are much larger—up to 100 feet (30 meters) around the base.

Many of these giant trees are several thousand years old. None has been known to die of old age, disease, or insect attack. However, lightning has destroyed the tops of the largest sequoia trees.

The General Sherman Tree is the world's largest tree. This giant sequoia has been growing for 2,200 to 2,500 years. It can be seen in Sequoia National Park, California.

Lost Tree Found

Until recently, scientists believed that the dawn redwood tree had died out 20 million years ago. They knew the tree only from its fossil remains. But in 1941, a Chinese forester found a large tree in a hidden valley. In 1946, it was identified as a dawn redwood. Other living dawn redwoods were found in several areas of China. Today, trees raised from the seeds of these trees grow in the United States.

The rafflesia *(ra FLEE zhuh)* of Southeast Asia is the world's largest flower. It can measure more than 3 feet (90 centimeters) wide. Rafflesias have no stems or leaves. Their flowers usually have a bad odor that attracts flies and beetles, which pollinate the flowers.

The Gondwana Rainforests of Australia include the largest areas of subtropical rain forest in the world. The rain forests are home to more than 100 rare or threatened plant species.

Plants are the oldest living things. This Great Basin bristlecone pine is an ancient resident of California. Some of these trees have lived for more than 4,000 years. They're as old as the pyramids of Egypt!

Few plants can live in deserts. Yet deserts have some of the most fantastic scenery in the world. There are hot deserts, cold deserts, and even a "painted" desert. It is a wonder that any life can exist in deserts, but it does.

Alive in the desert

Deserts are dry because rainfall is scarce, but they are not wastelands. Deserts have varied landscapes, and many kinds of animals and plants manage to live in them.

The roots of desert plants reach deep underground to find water. Some plants can store water in their leaves, roots, or stems. Desert plants grow and flower quickly after rainfall, making the desert suddenly bright with color.

Many desert animals come out in the cool of night. To escape the daytime heat, they rest in the shade, or dig burrows (underground holes).

The saguaro is the largest cactus of the United States. It may stand as tall as 60 feet (18 meters). The saguaro grows only in the foothills and deserts of southern Arizona, southeastern California, and northwestern Mexico.

The Painted Desert of Arizona is famous for the blues, reds, and yellows of its rocky landscape. The colors, caused by **minerals** in the rocks, are most brilliant at sunrise and sunset.

The Great Sahara

The Sahara in northern Africa is the world's largest desert. It is roughly as big as the United States! The Sahara was not always dry. About 10,000 years ago, its climate was much wetter. Elephants, giraffes, and many other animals roamed its grasslands and forests. About 6,000 years ago, the climate became drier and the Sahara region began turning into a desert.

Sand and palm trees

Travelers in sandy deserts marvel at the giant ridges of windblown sand called dunes. In the Sahara, large seas of sand called ergs form dunes 600 feet (180 meters) high. Travelers seek the cool shade of palm trees at an oasis—a **fertile** area where underground water feeds wells and springs, allowing plants to grow.

Shifting Sands

Great Sand Dunes National Monument has been called one of the strangest natural wonders in the United States. This huge stretch of sand, at the base of the Sangre de Cristo Mountains in Colorado, is constantly shifting. Sometimes it forms dunes that are 750 feet (230 meters) tall.

Fennec foxes live in the deserts of northern Africa and the Arabian Peninsula. The foxes' light coloring keeps them cool in the daytime heat and helps them blend into the sand to avoid hunting animals.

Deserts **41**

Ice on the Move

In the frozen regions of the world, ice and snow cover large areas of land and ocean. There are moving rivers of ice—and icebergs as big as islands. In the Antarctic, the ice is thick enough to bury the tallest skyscrapers!

Antarctic icebox

About 70 percent of the world's fresh water lies frozen in the Antarctic icecap—a thick layer of ice and snow that covers most of the great southern continent. If that ice melted, the water level of the oceans would rise and flood coastal cities around the world.

Downhill all the way

A glacier is a large mass of ice that flows slowly downhill over land. Glaciers are found in the cold polar regions and high in mountain valleys, where it is so cold that thick snow builds up and turns to ice. The ice in some glaciers is 10,000 feet (3,000 meters) thick.

Most glaciers move slowly—about 1 inch (2.5 centimeters) or so a day. But some glaciers can sprint 100 feet (30 meters) in a day.

A glacier flows from the Juneau Icefield in Alaska. Melting ice forms a lake at the end of the glacier.

Icebergs

When a glacier reaches the sea, huge masses of ice may break off the lower end and crash into the ocean to become icebergs. Explorers have written descriptions of icebergs that compare them to towers, pyramids, cathedrals, and palaces.

Although an iceberg may tower 400 feet (120 meters) above the surface of the ocean, this is only a small part—one-seventh to one-tenth—of the whole. Most of an iceberg is hidden below the surface of the water.

In Antarctica, huge glaciers flow into the sea. Massive chunks of ice break off from the glaciers to form icebergs.

Polar bears hunt for seals along the floating ice. In recent years, global warming has reduced the ice on which the bears live and hunt, threatening their survival.

Carved in Rock

A memorial is something that serves as a reminder of some event or person, such as a statue, a book, a holiday, or a park. Since ancient times, people have made memorials and statues of rock, hoping they would withstand the passing of time. Around the world, there are many amazing stone figures that often took years to complete.

Mount Rushmore

Mount Rushmore National Memorial is a huge carving on a granite cliff in the Black Hills of South Dakota. The carving, designed by sculptor Gutzon Borglum, depicts four great American presidents. Workers used models one-twelfth actual size to help create the figures. Carving the giant sculptures out of the cliff began in 1927 and ended more than 14 years later.

The Mount Rushmore National Memorial has the largest figures of any statue in the world. The head of George Washington (farthest left of the four) is as high as a five-story building. The other heads (left to right) are likenesses of Thomas Jefferson, Theodore Roosevelt, and Abraham Lincoln.

Huge figures depicting Buddha and his attendants were cut from solid rock by Asian sculptors for a cliffside chapel at a cave in east-central China.

Easter Island's statues

Easter Island, a small island in the South Pacific Ocean, is famous for the enormous statues that its people carved hundreds of years ago. More than 600 statues are scattered around the island. The tallest are 40 feet (12 meters) high.

The figures were carved from the rock of an extinct volcano and set up on raised **temple** platforms. Huge red stone cylinders balance on the heads of some of the statues, like hats. Even with modern methods, it would be difficult to erect such large statues and balance cylinders on top of them.

The figures may have been built to honor ancestors (relatives from long ago). The people who made these impressive figures settled on Easter Island between about A.D. 900 and 1200. The settlers were Polynesians who sailed to the remote island from islands to the west.

An unfinished gigantic sculpture of Crazy Horse, a leader of a band of Lakota Indians, is being carved out of a mountain in the Black Hills in South Dakota. Work began on what is to be the world's biggest sculpture in 1948.

Mysterious stone statues on Easter Island were carved hundreds of years ago.

Bridges and Dams

Bridges and dams are wonders of engineering. Modern engineers have built bridges and dams higher and longer than ever before.

Brooklyn Bridge is a suspension bridge over the East River in New York City. It was opened in 1883.

Concrete giant

Shasta Dam in California is one of the highest gravity dams in the United States. Gravity dams hold back the force of water behind them with their own weight alone. These dams are the strongest and most massive dams built today.

The "Eighth Wonder of the World"

This was the proud title given to the Brooklyn Bridge—the longest suspension bridge in the world when it was completed in 1883. A suspension bridge has its roadway hung on cables and chains between towers. The Brooklyn Bridge extends 1,595 feet (486 meters) across New York City's East River. It was built to connect the boroughs of Brooklyn and Manhattan.

Spanning the entrance to San Francisco Bay, the Golden Gate Bridge is one of the most famous and beautiful suspension bridges in the world.

High Wires

The world's longest bridges are suspension bridges. In a suspension bridge, the roadway hangs from steel cables slung between two towers. Suspension bridges are used to cross long distances. Most suspension bridges are more than 1,000 feet (300 meters) long. They can be built over deep water or steep canyons because they need only two piers, each of which supports a tower.

The Golden Gate Bridge

The towers of the Golden Gate Bridge can be seen from ships approaching San Francisco. This bridge is one of the largest and most spectacular suspension bridges in the world. The distance between the two towers is 4,200 feet (1,280 meters), and the total length of the bridge is 8,981 feet (2,737 meters).

The Golden Gate Bridge opened in 1937 to carry traffic across a channel of San Francisco Bay. Cars, trucks, and people on foot cross the bridge 220 feet (67 meters) above the water.

Liberty and the Tower

The Statue of Liberty is one of the largest statues ever built. This figure of a robed woman holding a torch towers above Liberty Island at the entrance to New York Harbor.

The Statue of Liberty towers above Liberty Island at the entrance to New York Harbor. It is a symbol of the United States. It was also a symbol of freedom for immigrants arriving by ship.

A gift from France

The Statue of Liberty was a gift to the people of the United States from the people of France in 1884. It was dedicated at a grand opening ceremony in 1886. The French sculptor Frédéric Auguste Bartholdi designed and built the figure as a **monument** to American independence.

Copper skin, iron bones

The figure of Liberty is made of 300 sheets of copper. The French **engineer** Gustave Eiffel *(EYE fuhl)* designed an iron and steel "skeleton" to support Liberty's thin copper skin. With this strong but flexible framework, the statue can withstand fierce winds. Liberty stands on a granite and concrete pedestal (base) 154 feet (47 meters) high.

Starts and stops

French workers began to shape the figure in 1875. By 1884, Liberty was complete, but it was still in France. In America, work on the pedestal stopped when money ran out, but a newspaper campaign saved the project. The pedestal was finished in April 1886.

Liberty Facts

- The statue stands 151 feet, 1 inch (46.05 meters) high from its feet to the top of the torch. It weighs 225 tons (204 metric tons).
- Inside the statue are two spiral stairways with 142 steps.
- The torch towers 305 feet, 1 inch (92.99 meters) above the base of the pedestal.
- Liberty got a new torch in 1986 as part of restoration work.

Liberty sails to America

The statue was then taken apart and packed into crates for shipment across the Atlantic Ocean. President Grover Cleveland led the celebration of the statue's arrival at the opening ceremony on October 28, 1886.

Construction of the Statue of Liberty began in Paris in 1875. The statue was shipped to the United States in 1886.

Eiffel's Tower

In 1889, people visiting a world's fair in Paris marveled at the sight of an iron and steel tower. The tower rose 984 feet (300 meters) above the ground, the world's tallest structure at that time.

Gustave Eiffel built his tower to show how iron and steel could be used for tall structures. The money he raised to pay for the tower was quickly repaid, as about 2 million people paid to visit the Eiffel Tower in the first year. The Eiffel Tower is still the most famous landmark in Paris.

The Eiffel Tower stands in a park called the Champ de Mars, near the Seine River. The structure includes observation decks and restaurants.

Sights to See

People today travel the world to see its most spectacular buildings. Some buildings are recent wonders, such as skyscrapers. Others are magnificent structures that have survived many centuries.

The Parthenon temple stands above Athens on a hill known as the Acropolis.

The Parthenon

The ancient Greeks built many **temples.** They generally chose a site on a hill overlooking a city. Such a site was known as an acropolis *(uh KROP uh lihs)*.

The most famous acropolis is on a rocky hilltop in Athens, capital of Greece. There, the Athenians *(uh THEE nee uhns)* built a magnificent group of temples. Among them was the Parthenon, built between 447 and 432 B.C., and dedicated to the goddess Athena. Many people think that the Parthenon and other ruined temples on the Acropolis in Athens are among the most beautiful buildings ever constructed.

The Colosseum

The Colosseum, the largest outdoor theater in ancient Rome, is now one of the world's most famous **ruins.** Built of brick and concrete, with stone covering the outside, it has four stories and is oval in shape. When completed in A.D. 80, the Colosseum could seat about 50,000 people on marble and wooden benches.

Roman crowds packed the Colosseum to watch mock naval battles, combat between gladiators (trained warriors), and fights between men and wild animals. Later, the Colosseum fell into ruins, and many of its stones were carried off to be used in new buildings.

The Colosseum is a huge arena in Rome. Damaged by an earthquake in the 1300's, the Colosseum was for many years mined for stone used in other buildings.

victories in battle. They were also great builders who perfected the arch—a curved structure that supports or strengthens a building.

The most famous arch in Rome is the Arch of Constantine, built about 315. The arch honored the victory of Emperor Constantine, who defeated a rival (competitor) for power and became ruler of the western part of the Roman Empire in 312.

The Pont du Gard

The ancient Romans also built many aqueducts *(AK wuh duhkts)*—channels that carry water from one place to another. Aqueducts supplied Rome and other cities with water.

The Pont du Gard, an aqueduct near Nîmes in France, is one of the most impressive examples of Roman **engineering** skill. Arches on three levels supported a water-carrying channel. The aqueduct is 2,000 years old and still draws many admiring visitors.

The Arch of Constantine was built as a tribute to the Roman Emperor Constantine. The Romans built similar arches in cities throughout their empire.

The Pont du Gard in southern France is a magnificent example of ancient engineering skill. ⌄

Saint Basil's Cathedral

Every visitor to Moscow, the capital of Russia, recognizes Saint Basil's Cathedral, the city's most famous church. Its colorful, onion-shaped spires (top parts of towers) rise into the sky above Red Square. The cathedral was built more than 400 years ago to celebrate Russian conquests. Later, it became a museum. Nearby stands the Kremlin, the grim fortress (place built with walls and defenses) within whose walls are richly decorated churches, palaces, and government buildings still in use.

Saint Basil, for whom the cathedral is named, lived from about 330 to 379. He was a leader of the early Christian Church in the East.

Saint Basil's Cathedral in Moscow is one of the Russian capital's best-known landmarks.

How far can it lean? Pisa's famous tower has been tilting for more than 600 years.

The Leaning Tower of Pisa

Straighten up! Seeing Pisa's *(PEE zuh's)* most celebrated building makes people think this town in Italy is sliding sideways.

The Leaning Tower was built as a bell tower for Pisa Cathedral. Construction lasted from 1173 to about 1370, but the builders had chosen a poor site. The land beneath the tower is a mixture of sand, clay, and water. After the first three stories were built, the soft ground started to sink, and the tower began leaning.

In 1990, the tower was closed for repairs. At that time, its lean had been increasing an average of $\frac{1}{20}$ of an inch (1.3 millimeters) per year. **Engineers** stabilized the tower's foundation and straightened it about 15 inches (38 centimeters) to prevent it from eventually collapsing. Today it is 14 ½ feet (4.4 meters) out of line when measured from the seventh story. The tower was reopened to the public in 2001.

The Taj Mahal

It has been called "the most beautiful building in the world." The Taj Mahal *(TAHJ muh HAHL)* is a white marble **tomb** at Agra in northern India. The Indian ruler Shah Jahan *(SHAH juh HAHN)* ordered it built for his wife Mumtaz Mahal, who died in 1629. About 20,000 workers built the Taj Mahal between 1630 and 1650.

City on the sea

Venice is a city with no highways. People go to work by boat on the city's canals (man-made waterways). Venice covers about 120 islands off the coast of Italy, at the north end of the Adriatic Sea. The city has more than 150 canals. Majestic palaces built between the 1100's and 1800's line the Grand Canal—the city's main waterway.

At the heart of Venice is Saint Mark's Square. Here, a bell tower called the Campanile *(kam puh NEE lay)* rises above the Basilica of Saint Mark, a 900-year-old church. Next to the Basilica is the Doges' Palace, home of the rulers of Venice, who were called doges *(dohj es)*.

Venice was once a rich city-state, an independent city that governed itself and its surrounding villages and farmland. Priceless works of art may be seen all over this wonderful city. However, Venice has its problems. Floods weaken its old buildings, and air pollution (dirt and waste) damages its art treasures. Some people fear that Venice may one day sink beneath the waters that make it unique.

The Taj Mahal is designed so that all four sides of the building look the same. Gardens surround the structure. Beneath the great dome, Shah Jahan and his wife lie together in a mausoleum.

Venice is one of the world's most famous and unusual cities. It has canals instead of streets. Its people use boats instead of automobiles, buses, taxis, and trucks.

Sydney Opera House

Opened in 1973, the Opera House beside Sydney Harbour is probably Australia's most famous building. The billowing white "sails" of the roof make it look as if the building is about to sail out into Sydney Harbour. The Opera House is a center for music, drama, and ballet, as well as for opera. Many people think it is one of the great buildings of the 20th century.

Landmarks of Toronto

Visitors to Toronto in Canada marvel at the CN (Canadian National) Tower—one of the world's tallest free-standing structures. This concrete-and-steel broadcasting tower soars 1,815 feet (553 meters) above the city. From the observation deck near the top, people enjoy breathtaking views and can peer down on the nearby Rogers Centre, an impressive sports stadium with a roof that opens and closes. The Rogers Centre is home to Toronto's baseball and football teams.

Sydney Opera House is one of the finest buildings of modern times. It was designed by Danish architect Jørn Utzon.

The CN Tower in Toronto is a giant needle pointing skyward. Beside it is the Rogers Centre.

Higher and Higher

- The Home Insurance Building (1884-1885) in Chicago was a well-known "ancestor" of the modern skyscraper. This 10-story building was torn down in 1931.
- The world's most famous skyscraper is probably the Empire State Building in New York City. From 1931 until the 1970's, it was the world's tallest building. The Empire State Building has 102 stories and soars 1,250 feet (381 meters) from the ground to the rooftop.
- The Burj Khalifa (Khalifa Tower) in Dubai, which opened in 2010, is the world's tallest building at a height of 2,684 feet (818 meters).

How High Is High?

The heights of skyscrapers given here are a measure of the distance from the ground to the building's top. They do not include broadcasting antennas that add extra height.

Reach for the sky

Architects in Chicago developed the skyscraper in the late 1800's. They stripped away the heavy walls of stone and brick that supported tall buildings. Instead, they designed structures with steel skeletons, which allowed buildings to soar to great heights and yet look light and graceful.

The Willis Tower, formerly known as the Sears Tower, was the world's tallest building when completed in 1973. Its 110 stories rise 1,450 feet (442 meters) above the ground.

The Willis Tower in Chicago was the tallest building in the United States when completed. It includes an all-glass observation deck that offers striking views of the city.

The Burj Khalifa (Khalifa Tower) in Dubai is the world's tallest building. ❯

Ancient Riddles

Some of the world's wonders are baffling. How and why were they built? And how did they come to be as they are today?

One of Cleopatra's Needles stands in Central Park in New York City.

Stonehenge

Stonehenge, an ancient **monument** on Salisbury Plain in southwest England, is a group of huge rough-cut stones set in circles. There are other stone circles in the United Kingdom, but Stonehenge is the most famous.

Experts believe that ancient peoples began building Stonehenge about 3100 B.C. The people who dragged the heavy stones to the site and heaved them into place were building something of great importance— a tribal gathering place and religious center. The stones were set in place with care and were probably used as a "clock" to forecast such events as the rising and setting of the sun on a midsummer day.

Today, Stonehenge is a popular tourist attraction. It has been designated a World Heritage site, an area of unique natural or cultural importance. ➤

Cleopatra's Needles

Today, two famous obelisks (pillars of stone) from ancient Egypt stand in New York City's Central Park and beside the River Thames in London. These famous stones, called Cleopatra's Needles, were gifts from Egypt to the United States and the United Kingdom in the 1870's.

Rulers of ancient Egypt set up obelisks as monuments to the sun god Re *(ray)*. The New York obelisk is 69 feet (21 meters) high; the London obelisk is slightly smaller.

Both stones are more than 3,000 years old. They are marked with writing bearing the names of kings who ruled Egypt during the 1400's and 1200's B.C. Nobody knows why they are associated with Cleopatra, a much later queen of Egypt.

Great Serpent Mound

If you were in a plane flying low over the trees near Hillsboro, Ohio, you would see what looks like a huge snake coiled on the ground. The "snake" is a mound of earth made more than 2,000 years ago by Native Americans. Called Great Serpent Mound, it was built by the Adena people of Ohio as a burial place. The mound grew bigger as more bodies were added to it, and it now measures more than ¼ mile (0.4 kilometer) long. Thousands of such ancient burial mounds can still be seen in Canada and the United States.

Great Serpent Mound was made by Native Americans in Ohio.

Over millions of years, Earth's processes have formed some of the most striking wonders of the world.

Tree stumps of stone

At Florissant Fossil Beds National Monument in Colorado, people stop to gaze at a fossilized tree stump. They can also see fossilized insects, leaves, and seeds that date back about 35 million years.

Petrified forest

A petrified forest isn't scared stiff, but it is definitely solid! Here stand the remains of tree trunks that were buried in mud, sand, or volcanic ash ages ago, and gradually turned into stone. **Mineral**-bearing water seeped into the wood as it decayed, creating a stone replica of the original log.

The remains of pine tree logs that are now part of Petrified Forest National Park in Arizona were washed downstream by river waters about 225 million years ago.

Fossilized tree stumps are the remains of trees that lived millions of years ago. They form after being buried in mud, sand, or volcanic ash.

Petrified Forest National Park lies in the Painted Desert in northeastern Arizona. The park contains one of the greatest and most colorful concentrations of petrified wood in the world.

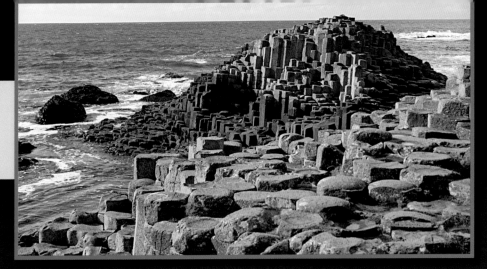

A bridge made for giants? Scientists say the Giant's Causeway in Ireland is an unusual volcanic rock formation.

Irish giant

The Giant's Causeway is a natural wonder of Northern Ireland, where about 40,000 columns of a hard, dark volcanic rock called basalt stand grouped together on the coast of County Antrim. This strange rock formation gets its name from an old legend. Finn MacCool, the hero of many Irish tales, built the causeway across the sea channel from Ireland to Scotland so that giants could pass over it. Scientists believe the causeway was formed from volcanic lava.

Wind shapes

Erosion—the wearing away of rock by wind, water, and sand—can change landscapes and create unusual shapes. Sand blowing across the desert sculpted Delicate Arch in Utah from a wall of ancient **sandstone.**

Delicate Arch in Utah is an example of how wind can wear away rock. The softer rock is worn away first, leaving a hole. Over thousands of years, a natural arch is created.

Wonders and Mysteries

Some wonders are revealed to us only through a microscope. Others are locked away, under guard, because they are so valuable. Still others are there for all to see or touch, and yet they remain mysteries.

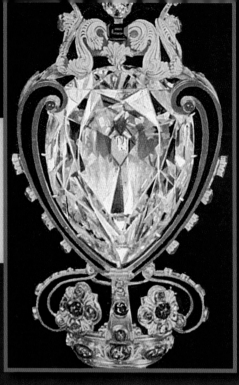

The Star of Africa is the world's largest cut diamond.

Jewel in the crown

Diamonds—precious stones that are crystals of the chemical element carbon—have been treasured throughout history. They are the hardest substance in nature—the most lasting gemstones and the most valued. When a diamond is cut to produce many facets (sides) and polished, it reflects light brilliantly. The facets break up light into the colors of the rainbow.

The largest natural diamond ever discovered was the Cullinan diamond, found in a South African mine in 1905. It weighed 3,106 carats, or about 1 ⅓ pounds (0.6 kilogram). This huge stone, given to King Edward VII of the United Kingdom, was cut into 9 large gems and 96 smaller stones. From it came the Star of Africa, the largest flawless cut diamond in the world and now part of the British Crown Jewels.

Ice from the sky

The largest hailstone ever recorded in the United States fell on July 23, 2010, in Vivian, South Dakota. The hailstone measured 8 inches (about 20 centimeters) wide.

A resident of Vivian, South Dakota, discovered a record-breaking hailstone in 2010 after a strong thunderstorm swept across the land.

The Willamette meteorite was discovered in Oregon in 1902.

Rock from space

The Willamette meteorite, a big chunk of iron from space, is the largest meteorite ever found in the United States. It is 118 inches (287 centimeters) long, weighs about 15 ½ tons (14 metric tons), and was found in the Willamette Valley, Oregon, in 1902. In 1920, an even bigger space rock was discovered in Namibia, southwestern Africa. It is the largest meteorite ever found, weighing about 66 tons (60 metric tons).

Nearly all snow crystals have six sides, but they vary in shape.

Patterns in ice

Some natural wonders would remain unknown without the lenses of high-powered cameras and microscopes. The snow crystal shown on this page was photographed with a microscope.

Stuck in!

Amber is the hard fossilized resin of pine trees that grew millions of years ago. The resins were gummy materials mixed with oils in the trees. When the dead trees decayed underground or in water, the resin slowly changed into lumps of amber. Some lumps contain air bubbles or insects that became trapped in the sticky resin.

Amber is a substance made from trees that grew in prehistoric times.

archaeologist a person who studies the people, customs, and life of long ago.

chariot a two-wheeled cart in which the driver stands.

civilization; civilized a society highly developed in its systems of government, agriculture, arts, and sciences; advanced in social customs, art, and science

engineer; engineering a person who plans and builds engines, machines, roads, bridges, canals, or the like; the use of science to design structures, machines, and products.

fertile rich in things that aid growth and development.

limestone a light-colored rock used for building. Marble is a form of limestone.

mineral a solid, natural substance that is not a plant or animal, and which was never alive.

monument a stone, statue, or other structure set up to show respect for an important person or event.

Persian Empire an ancient empire that was founded in about 550 B.C. by Cyrus II. The empire lasted about 200 years and was based in parts of what are now Iran and Afghanistan.

Roman of or having to do with ancient Rome or its people. The Roman Empire controlled most of Europe and the Middle East from 27 B.C. to A.D. 476.

ruin something left after destruction, decay, or downfall, especially a building or wall that has fallen to pieces.

sacred having to do with God or a god.

sandstone a kind of rock made up of many grains of sand stuck together.

temple a building used for religious worship.

tomb a grave, building, or special room in which a dead body is placed.

Books

If Stones Could Speak: Unlocking the Secrets of Stonehenge by Marc Aronson and Michael Parker Pearson (National Geographic, 2010)

Easter Island: Giant Stone Statues Tell of a Rich and Tragic Past by Caroline Arnold (Clarion Books, 2000)

The Great Wall by Elizabeth Mann and Alan Witschonke (Mikaya Press, 1997)

Mount Everest by Jill Kalz (Creative Education, 2004)

Pyramid by Peter Chrisp (DK Publishing, 2006)

Secrets of the Sphinx by James Giblin and Bagram Ibatoulline (Scholastic Press, 2004)

Seven Natural Wonders of North America by Michael Woods and Mary B. Woods (Twenty-First Century Books, 2009)

Seven Wonders of the Ancient World by Lynn Curlee (Atheneum Books for Young Readers, 2002)

Wonders of the World by Philip Steele (Kingfisher, 2007)

Websites

Egypt: Secrets of an Ancient World
http://www.nationalgeographic.com/pyramids/pyramids.html

Timelines, diagrams, and images guide readers through the history of the Egyptian pyramids—the oldest, the largest, the last—at this educational website.

Everest: Beyond the Limit
http://dsc.discovery.com/convergence/everest/interactive/interactive.html

On this website, take a three-dimensional virtual tour of the world's highest mountain peak, and meet the people who've climbed Everest.

National Park Service: Grand Canyon
http://www.nps.gov/grca/index.htm

Podcasts, photo galleries, and webcams showcase the beauty of this natural wonder, which is now a national park.

NOVA: Secrets of the Parthenon
http://www.pbs.org/wgbh/nova/parthenon/

This website features an interactive look at the restoration of this ancient wonder, along with interviews and a tour of the building's many roles throughout the ages.

Pompeii: Stories from an Eruption
http://www.fieldmuseum.org/pompeii/index.html

Use an interactive timeline to relive the destruction of Pompeii and Herculaneum, as well as their rediscovery and preservation.

The Theban Mapping Project
http://www.thebanmappingproject.com/

At this website, interactive atlases serve as a guide to the tombs of the Valley of the Kings, as well as other ancient Egyptian monuments.

Savage Earth: Out of the Inferno
http://www.pbs.org/wnet/savageearth/volcanoes/index.html

Visit this website for information on such volcanoes as Mt. Saint Helens, Krakatau, Paricutín, and others.

Seven Ancient Wonders of the World
http://www.history.com/topics/seven-ancient-wonders-of-the-world

Watch videos about each of the seven ancient wonders at this website, which also features articles and links to more information.